LIFE ON

THE
RAILWAY

ANTHONY BURTON

IMPORTANT DATES

1804   The first public demonstration of a steam locomotive running on rails. Designed by Richard Trevithick, it ran on the Penydarren tramway in South Wales.

1808   Trevithick's locomotive *Catch-me-who-can* gives the first passenger rides on a circular track in London.

1812   The first commercial steam railway opens at Middleton Colliery near Leeds.

1814   George Stephenson builds his first locomotive, *Blücher*, for the Killingworth Colliery railway, near Newcastle upon Tyne.

1825   Opening of the Stockton & Darlington Railway, the first public railway to be built for use by steam locomotives.

1830   Opening of the Liverpool & Manchester Railway, the first to use locomotives for both freight and passengers, and scene of the first fatal railway accident.

1836   The opening of the 23½ in (approximately 0.6m) Ffestiniog Railway in Wales, the first narrow gauge to be converted to steam.

1838   The opening of Brunel's broad-gauge Great Western Railway (GWR) between London and Bristol.

1841   Thomas Cook runs the first railway excursion train from Leicester to Loughborough; electric telegraph first used with signals.

1863   The world's first underground railway opens in London.

1873   The first sleeping car introduced by North British Railways between London and Glasgow and Edinburgh.

1879   The Tay railway bridge in Scotland collapses with the loss of 78 lives.

1883   Opening of Volk's Railway at Brighton – Britain's first electric railway.

1904   *City of Truro* becomes the first locomotive to travel at over 100mph (160kph).

1923   A total of 123 separate railway companies are amalgamated to form four groups: London, Midland and Scottish (LMS), London & North Eastern Railway (LNER), Great Western Railway (GWR) and Southern.

1938   The A4 locomotive *Mallard* sets a world speed record for steam locomotives of 126mph (203kph), a record that still stands.

1948   The railways are nationalized.

1960   *Evening Star* is the last steam locomotive to be built by British Railways.

1993   Railways are privatized, and divided between one organization responsible for infrastructure and separate companies to run the trains.

2013   The London Underground celebrates its 150th anniversary.

➤   An admission ticket to see *Catch-me-who-can,* with notes written round the margin by Trevithick's friend Davies Gilbert, the renowned scientist.

THE FIRST RAILWAYS

By the end of the 18th century there were a considerable number of railways in Britain, most of them linking industrial sites, such as collieries, to navigable rivers and canals. They were generally known as tramways, and horses were used to pull the trucks along. By this time steam engines were well established and used for many tasks, from pumping water from mines to providing power for textile mills. They all used steam at low pressure: if more power was needed, a bigger engine had to be built – and some were enormous, with cylinders 6 feet (1.8m) or more in diameter, and as high as a two-storey building.

It was a brilliant young Cornish mining engineer named Richard Trevithick, itching to find new ways of using steam, who realized that the other way to get more power was to increase steam pressure, and he was able to build portable engines that could be pulled along by horses. Then he went a stage further and decided to build an engine that would move itself: a locomotive. His new engine was given its first outing on the road at Camborne in Cornwall on Christmas Eve 1801. Its career was short-lived: four days later it ran off the road and its boiler exploded. Trevithick failed to interest anyone in steam road carriages, so in 1804 he built an engine to run on the rails of the Penydarren tramway that served an iron works in the Welsh town of Merthyr Tydfil. He wrote: 'It works exceeding well, and is much more manageable than horses.' But it broke the rails. Trevithick made one last attempt to sell his idea when he ran another locomotive, *Catch-me-who-can*, for paying passengers in London. When that failed, he gave up and left it to others to continue what he had started.

▲ Richard Trevithick's locomotive *Catch-me-who-can* gave passengers rides, for which they paid one shilling (5p), on a circular track near the site of the present Euston station in London.

▲ The world's first successful commercial steam railway, built for the Middleton Colliery. A typical miner of the period is in the foreground.

Although Richard Trevithick's engines worked well, the fact that they smashed the rails made them unusable. Industrialists decided to continue using horses, until the Napoleonic wars sent the price of fodder rocketing. John Blenkinsop of Middleton Colliery near Leeds in Yorkshire pondered the problem. A light engine would not break the rails but nor could it do the job. What was needed was extra traction. Together with a Leeds engineer, Matthew Murray, Blenkinsop came up with a solution: the rack and pinion, where a toothed wheel on the engine engaged with a cogged rail – the sort of device now only seen on mountain railways. The Middleton Colliery railway, opened in 1812, was highly successful and several people made special trips to see it, including a young enginewright from Killingworth Colliery in Northumberland by the name of George Stephenson.

GEORGE STEPHENSON

Stephenson was encouraged by his employers to build a locomotive for their colliery and the resulting engine, the *Blücher*, was closely modelled on the Middleton engine, but without the rack and pinion. Stephenson was not, however, the first engineer from the north-east to build a locomotive to serve a local colliery – that honour went to William Hedley – but he was the most important. He became a champion of the steam locomotive, and was successful in persuading promoters to build a public railway between Stockton and Darlington that would use steam locomotives for freight. His first engine for the new line was *Locomotion*, built in 1825. It was typical of early engines and driving it was quite unlike anything on later engines. The driver stood on a wooden platform at the side of the engine, with connecting rods going up and down in front of his nose. It had no reversing mechanism, so he had to see where the piston was in the cylinder, unclip the valve gear to move the connecting rods in the right direction, and put it together again when it was moving. The line also carried passengers, but they had to make do with a stagecoach with flanged wheels pulled by horses.

LIKE FATHER, LIKE SON

The opening of the Stockton & Darlington was important, but not everyone was convinced that steam locomotives were the best machines for

George Stephenson (1781–1848) pictured in the days of his success. In the background a train crosses Chat Moss, a section of boggy ground on the Liverpool & Manchester Railway that gave the engineer a great deal of trouble.

nning a railway. George Stephenson was invited o survey a line to join Liverpool to Manchester, ut the proprietors were undecided whether to use ocomotives or to have a series of stationary engines read along the route, hauling trains in between by ables. They offered a prize of £500 to anyone who uld design an engine that could haul a train of rriages weighing 20 tons for the whole length of the e at a speed of 10mph (16kph). There were three ain contestants. *Novelty* was a lightweight engine at looked very racy and was the popular favourite. ephenson rightly summed it up: 'no guts'. It failed. ans Pareil was a conventional colliery-type engine

The decision on whether or not to use steam locomotives for the Liverpool & Manchester Railway was decided by a trial at Rainhill, Lancashire, in 1829 between these three locomotives. *Rocket* was the winner.

William Hadley built this locomotive, *Wylam Dilly*, for the Wylam Colliery in 1813. It survived to be photographed half a century later with Hadley's sons posing beside the engine.

designed by Timothy Hackworth, but it too failed. The winner was *Rocket*, designed by Stephenson's son Robert, which had all the main design features that would appear in steam locomotives for decades to come. With its success, the Railway Age was born.

NAVVIES

We tend to think of station staff and train crews as being the people who worked on the railways, but there was another huge army of men at work right up to the end of the 19th century. These were the people who actually built the rail network, using nothing more sophisticated than spade, pickaxe and wheelbarrow – and strong muscles. They were the navvies, a name that was first used in the 18th century as an abbreviation of 'navigators' – the men who built canal navigations.

A HARD EXISTENCE

The navvies were full-time railway workers, moving from site to site and often living rough. They found accommodation where they could. In the 1851 census, an agricultural labourer and his family managed to find space in their cottage for 19 lodgers, made up of navvies and their families. When working out in the wild, as men did when building the Woodhead tunnel between Manchester and Sheffield, the men erected huts of dry-stone walls, covered them with thatch, and moved in with their own family, letting out space to 14 or 15 single men. Wives would tramp hundreds of miles with their husbands, carrying all their possessions as they moved around the country in order to find work.

The men were seldom employed directly by the railway companies, but were taken on by contractors, both large and small. Many, such as

Thomas Brassey who employed thousands of men, treated the navvies well, but some used the infamous 'truck' and 'tommy note' systems, instead of paying cash. 'Truck' involved giving the men goods instead of money, while with 'tommy' they got notes or tokens that could only be exchanged at the company stores. The system sometimes led

A navvy's wife outside the shack that was the family home during work on the Great Central Railway. The conditions on this line were far better than those on many others, where men had to build their own shacks out of whatever material they could find.

Such events made headlines in the newspapers, but they were by no means part of normal navvy life. It was certainly true that on paydays the navvies were liable to get drunk and take a day or two to recover, but mostly they were incredibly hard-working men. It was estimated that a navvy filling trucks with spoil would shift 20 tons a day, throwing it to a height of 6 feet (1.8m) to get it into the wagons. It was this exceptional physical strength that built the railways, with little or no help from machines.

to arguments that could turn into riots, earning navvies a reputation for riotous behaviour. Mostly, however, the serious riots developed when one group felt that another group had agreed to take work at a lower rate. For example, there was a full-scale battle between English and Irish navvies on the Great Western Railway in 1838, which ended with the army being called in. As a result, 24 navvies were sent to gaol.

➤ Barrow runs on the London & Birmingham Railway, as depicted by J.C. Bourne. The men can be seen balancing loaded barrows of spoil, which are being hauled up the planks by horses at the top of the bank.

▼ A group of navvies on one of the temporary tracks that were used to move basic materials around the construction sites.

It came as something of a surprise, even to the supporters of railways, to discover just how eager people were to travel on this new form of transport. The original promoters had thought of the Liverpool & Manchester Railway primarily as a freight line, and the enabling Act of Parliament had a wealth of clauses covering the rate that could be charged for all kinds of goods, and right at the end one saying 'For all Persons, Cattle and other Animals, such rates as the Company might decide upon'. In fact many people were treated little better than cattle. The poorer passengers travelled in what were simply open trucks fitted with planks for them to sit on, if they were lucky. Wealthier passengers often preferred to have their own coaches loaded onto flat wagons and they would stay in them for the duration of journey. Many were nervous about what might happen when travelling at such immense speeds as 30 miles (50km) an hour, and their fears were stoked by 'scientific experts', such as Dr Dionysus Lardner who proclaimed that a train passing through Box Tunnel in Wiltshire would 'deposit 3,090lbs [140kg] of noxious gases

FACING OPPOSITION

Not everyone welcomed the new railways. Some objected to the noise, the speed and the dirt, and others had stranger reasons. The Master of Jesus College, Cambridge, complained that 'they had made arrangements for conveying foreigners and others to Cambridge at such fares as might be likely to tempt persons who having no regard for Sunday themselves would inflict their presence on the University on that day of rest'.

incapable of supporting life'. As a result, the railway company found it necessary to arrange for a stop at the tunnel entrance to allow some passengers to get off and take a stagecoach over the top to rejoin the train at the other end. Other experts took a very different view: one doctor declared that rail travel was a boon that 'equalises the circulation, promotes digestion, tranquillises the nerves, and often causes sound sleep during the succeeding night'.

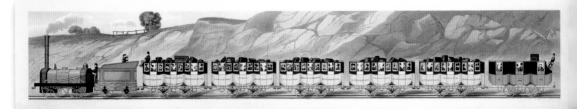

▲ Travel on the Liverpool & Manchester Railway in 1831. The illustration shows the locomotive *Jupiter*, hauling five first-class coaches and a mail coach. The guard sits on top of the first carriage.

▼ *North Star* hauling second-class coaches with overhead cover but open sides, with the very basic third-class at the rear.

△ Bath station in the 1850s. The gentry could arrange to take their own carriages on the train and many preferred to ride in those instead of in a compartment.

AILWAY TIME

he companies faced some problems not eviously experienced. For example, in Britain ocks were set to noon when the sun was at its ghest: but that meant that 12 noon in Bristol was ot the same as 12 noon in London. This was never problem with the old stagecoaches when journeys ok several days, but would have played havoc th the GWR timetables. So, in 1840, the company creed that all trains should run to London time. he guard leaving London would set his company atch and use it to adjust the clocks along the route what became known as 'Railway Time'.

TATION FACILITIES

rrangements also had to be made for people to ive a stop on long journeys, partly because they pected refreshments but, more importantly, ecause the trains had no toilet facilities. Every WR train had to make a compulsory stop at vindon, Wiltshire, where the refreshment room ined a certain notoriety for bad service. Brunel mself wrote to the manager that he 'was wrong supposing that I thought you purchased inferior offee. I thought I said to him I was surprised you tould buy such bad roasted corn'.

△ A train steaming into the mile-and-three-quarter (2.8km) long Box Tunnel. In the early years many passengers were too terrified to risk their lives by plunging through this great hole through the rocks.

△ The first-class refreshment room at Swindon in 1852. All trains made a compulsory stop here, though many passengers criticized the standards of the catering.

ON THE FOOTPLATE

▲ A Victorian driver standing beside his engine which, like all engines of that period, has no protection against the elements. The fireman is busy on the footplate.

▼ The crew of a London, Brighton & South Coast Railway locomotive, photographed from the tender in 1905. The driver is on the left, the fireman on the right. They have more protection from the weather than their Victorian counterparts.

Controlling a steam locomotive was the job of the footplate crew: the driver and the fireman who worked together as a team. The earliest drivers were recruited from among men who already had experience of handling stationary steam engines in mines and mills, but as well as being knowledgeable they also needed to be hardy types. The first locomotives had no cabs so the men were out in the open in all weathers. The railway companies deferred adding cabs for a long time, on the grounds that the men might get too comfortable and not pay attention to the job. That was hardly likely, for driving and firing steam engines were skilled and demanding jobs.

FIREMEN AND DRIVERS

Many small boys dreamed of being an engine driver, but it was not a job that was accessible to everyone. Would-be drivers started in the railway sheds, doing such mundane tasks as cleaning the engines. If they worked hard they might be promoted to firemen. Firing a locomotive was not comparable to looking after a domestic fire. A fireman had to be at the sheds early to light and tend his fire, so that there was enough steam to start the scheduled run. After that the general rule

r firing was 'little and often', keeping a good, even
e and the steam pressure just where it should
: too low and the engine struggled; too high and
e steam was wasted. When not shovelling coal,
e fireman was also responsible for checking on
ater levels in the boiler and helping the driver by
eping an eye on the train and on signals. It was
.id that no one could become a good driver unless
e had already been a good fireman.

he driver needed to have a complete knowledge
f the complex machine he had to control. His
ay started with a thorough inspection of the
ngine and a check that all equipment was in place.
he first essential for any good driver was that he
ould 'know the road' – that is, be aware of all the
radients and curves, know where the signals were
aced and be ready to react to them. Driving was
self a skilled occupation. A driver had two basic
ontrols: the regulator that controlled the supply
f steam to the cylinders, and the reverser that
ecided at what point in the cycle the steam was cut
ff. (A rough analogy would be the accelerator and
earshift of a motorcar.) To get the best out of his
ngine the driver had to work the two controls in
armony, and adjust them to suit the conditions.

▲ A fireman at work stoking a London, Midland and Scottish Class 5 locomotive. Designed in 1934, these were very popular all-purpose engines and over 800 of them were built.

The locomotive driver and fireman enjoyed a unique way of life. The footplate was their own little domain, with no one looking over their shoulders to tell them what to do and what not to do. They were masters of one of the most appealing machines ever built by man.

BREAKING THE RECORD

Driver Joe Duddington and fireman Tommy Bray were chosen to man the footplate of *Mallard* for an attempt on the British speed record of 114mph (183kph) on 3 July 1938. They broke the record,

but Duddington was not finished yet: 'Go on girl, I thought, we can do better than this. I nursed her and shot through Little Bytham at 123.' There was more to come: 'I accelerated up the bank at Stoke and passed Stoke box at 85. I gave *Mallard* her head and she jumped at it like a live thing.' At 4.36 p.m. they achieved the world record speed of 126mph (203kph).

➤ The crew of *Mallard* posing after the record-breaking run in 1938. They are (left to right) Tommy Bray, fireman, Joe Duddington, driver, and S. Jenkins, the inspector who recorded the speed.

THE RAILWAY GUARD

▲ The guard is giving the signal 'right away' by blowing his whistle and raising his flag to tell the driver it is now safe to start the train.

TRAVELLING POST OFFICES

One of the earliest innovations was the travelling post office. The first mail was carried on the Liverpool & Manchester Railway in 1837, but it was the Grand Junction Railway Company that introduced a special van on its route between Birmingham and Warrington the following year. This was a converted horsebox that not only carried the mail but also allowed it to be sorted en route. It had a mechanism, invented by a post

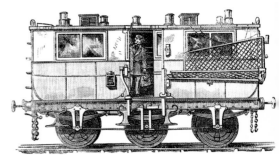

▲ A line drawing of a Victorian mail van in which post office workers sorted the mail during the journey. The net seen on the right would be swung out to pick up mailbags from the side of the track.

The other most important person after the footplate crew was the guard. In the very early days he had no special vehicle to ride in, but perched out in the open at the back of the rearmost carriage. In the days before there was any continuous braking system for trains, the only brakes were the one on the locomotive and a handbrake controlled by the guard. In an emergency – for example, if a coupling broke – he could bring the rest of the train to a safe halt. Later he was housed in his own guard's van, where he also kept a look out for signals and other dangers. The guard could communicate with the driver, and if he signalled that the train had to stop then the driver had to follow his instructions. It was a job of considerable responsibility. The guard's van also often doubled up as a parcel van: the guard would accept the different items and make sure that they were unloaded at the right station.

➤ A lady ticket collector on the GWR in 1917. During the First World War women were employed on trains for the first time because of the number of men who had left to join the army.

▶ A very handsome second-class buffet bar of the 1930s, with the staff smartly dressed in uniform.

▼ Luncheon cost four shillings (20p) when travelling on the Wolverhampton to Penzance line in 1921, as shown on this GWR menu.

office official, John Ramsey, that allowed the mailbags to be picked up and dropped at a trackside device while the train was moving. By the middle of the 20th century there were 73 travelling post offices at work, in which the staff sorted the post. It was a system made famous by the 1936 documentary film *Night Mail*, with its verse commentary written by W.H. Auden which starts: 'This is the Night Mail crossing the border, Bringing the cheque and the postal order ...'.

OTHER STAFF

The introduction of corridor trains that allowed people to move from compartment to compartment and carriage to carriage brought new staff to the trains. Ticket inspectors were now able to check tickets while the train was on the move, which made it far more difficult to avoid paying the fare. It had been possible to sleep on crude beds in carriages in the earliest days, but in 1873 proper sleeping cars were introduced, complete with attendants to make up the beds and look after passengers.

Another innovation was the introduction of the dining car on the Great Northern Railway's route between Leeds and London in 1879. Preheated meals had been served previously, but this dining car had its own kitchen producing excellent meals. The staff consisted of that of any restaurant, except that the chef and his assistants had the narrow confines of a kitchen that rocked and swayed, and the waiters had to provide exemplary service without pouring soup over a passenger's head when the train jolted.

Now when the guard waved his flag and blew his whistle to give the signal 'right away', there could be a sizeable staff working between him and the men on the footplate.

There were far more staff at railway stations in the 19th century than one would ever find today, and they had a great variety of jobs to attend to. We think of porters as being the men who carried passengers' luggage, but that was just one of their duties. Even when a passenger train arrived there were always goods to be loaded and unloaded from the guard's van – anything from mailbags to crates of homing pigeons. Handcarts would be lined up, piled with whatever needed to be loaded, and empty trucks would be waiting to take the unloaded goods. Everything had to be done quickly and efficiently to avoid delaying the train.

WORKING THE GOODS YARD

Loading and unloading was only a part of the work. Even quite modest country stations would have a goods yard, with a shed and sidings to hold trucks. It was a complicated system because customers would either deliver whatever they wanted carrying and expect trucks to be ready to take the goods, or privately owned wagons would be brought to the sidings. Then everything had to be put into order to make sure that the right trucks were attached to the correct trains. The trucks had to be shunted around and then coupled manually. Controlling the trucks as they rolled along under their own momentum was a skilled and potentially dangerous job, as was making sure that they were braked in time, so that the couplings could be put in place.

A USEFUL LESSON

'As a young porter, I was pleased when an experienced man showed me where to stand to be opposite the first-class carriage. The train arrived and I staggered to the taxi rank with two heavy cases and got a few coppers for my pains. The old porter, carrying one light suitcase for a third-class passenger, got silver in his hand. He smiled and told me: "Let that be a lesson to you, lad. Folk like them didn't get rich by giving it to folk like us."'

Anthony Burton, who worked at Harrogate station in the 1950s

▲ The staff of Colwyn Bay station posing for a picture in the 1920s. It is remarkable to see how many men were employed, but in 1904 the station was listed as being able to handle goods, passengers and parcels, furniture vans, livestock, horseboxes and personal carriages.

▲ This view of St Austell station in 1912 shows a passenger train at the platform, while a goods train is being connected to an assortment of trucks and vans in the sidings. Many stations had separate sections for passengers and freight.

▲ Railways had to deal with many customers who had their own wagons, as well as with the company's own rolling stock. Assembling everything in the right order was a complex business, and here a horse is being used to shunt a wagon.

▼ An important part of the work of station staff involved coupling carriages and wagons in the correct order to 'make up' the train.

REPORTING TO THE STATIONMASTER

There were plenty of other tasks to be done. Tickets had to be sold and collected. The collection was important, because in the days when a journey might involve travel over lines owned by several

▲ Porters were not just employed to carry passengers' luggage. This porter is busy unloading boxes of fish at Paddington in the early years of the 20th century.

different companies, all tickets had to go to a central clearing house to make sure everyone got their fair share of the price. Another familiar figure on the platform was the wheel tapper. He hit carriage wheels and if they emitted a tuneful ping all was well – but if the note was flat it indicated a crack and passengers had to get out and find seats somewhere else. Other jobs that have now disappeared included that of the lamp man who went down the line from the station replacing the oil lamps in the signals. And there was always office work to be done, from sticking labels on luggage to recording the movement of freight. Overseeing it all was the stationmaster, a grand figure in an imposing uniform, who usually enjoyed the privilege of having a comfortable home next to his station.

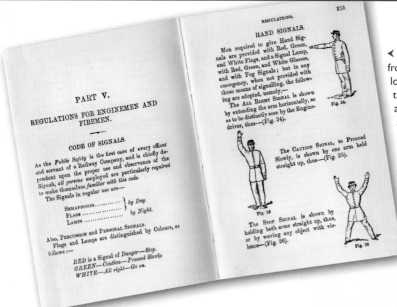

REGULATIONS.

235

HAND SIGNALS.

Men required to give Hand Signals are provided with Red, Green, and White Flags, and a Signal Lamp, with Red, Green, and White Glasses, and with Fog Signals; but in any emergency, when not provided with those means of signalling, the following are adopted, namely,—
The ALL RIGHT SIGNAL is shown by extending the arm horizontally, so as to be distinctly seen by the Engine-driver, thus—(Fig. 24).

The CAUTION SIGNAL, to Proceed Slowly, is shown by one arm held straight up, thus—(Fig. 25).

The STOP SIGNAL is shown by holding both arms straight up, thus, or by waving any object with violence—(Fig. 26).

Fig. 24.

Fig. 25.

Fig. 26.

PART V.

REGULATIONS FOR ENGINEMEN AND FIREMEN.

CODE OF SIGNALS.

As the *Public Safety* is the first care of every officer and servant of a Railway Company, and is chiefly dependent upon the proper use and observance of the Signals, all persons employed are particularly required to make themselves *familiar with this code.*
The Signals in regular use are—

SEMAPHORES............ } by Day.
FLAGS .... } by Day.
LAMPS .... by Night.

Also, PERCUSSION and PERSONAL SIGNALS.
Flags and Lamps are distinguished by Colours, as follows :—

RED is a Signal of Danger—*Stop.*
GREEN—*Caution—Proceed Slowly.*
WHITE—*All right—Go on.*

◄ Hand signals demonstration from a 19th-century handbook for locomotive drivers. They are, from top to bottom, 'All Right' (meaning all clear), 'Caution' (proceed slowly) and 'Stop'.

▼ An artist's impression of a railway signalman of the 1840s. At this time the men worked out in the open on raised platforms, operating the signals by a system of levers and pulleys.

On the roads, coaches and carts could overtake and manoeuvre round each other, but trains all had to use the same constricting track, so the railway companies were faced with the problem of how to avoid collisions. The first answer to this challenge was introduced on the Liverpool & Manchester Railway. They issued a rule stating that there must be a ten-minute gap between one train and the next, and this gap had to be maintained by the railway police, using hand signals or waving flags. This was slightly improved by hanging lamps on posts – a white light for 'go ahead' and a red light for 'stop'. This involved the signalman climbing to the top of the pole, changing the white light to red when a train went past, and going up again ten minutes later to change it back to white. It was not very satisfactory.

THE SIGNALMAN

By the 1840s, the first mechanical signals had been introduced, and at first the signalman was perched on a raised platform out in the open, using a lever to work the signals, but still relying on the time gap to control movement. The other problem facing the signalman was that he did not know what was going on further along the line. This was solved for the first time in 1838, when the GWR introduced an electric telegraph between Paddington and West Drayton in Middlesex. The idea soon spread and the next big improvement came in 1844 on

▲ A signalman 'pulling off' a signal, which alters the position of the signal on the track, at Exeter Middle signal box. This was a busy box controlling a large number of signals. The telegraph can be seen on the shelf above the levers.

NIGHT WORKS

When night-time came, the drivers still needed to be able to see the signals, so a system was developed that involved introducing coloured glass into the end of the familiar semaphore signal, and placing a lantern behind it. If, for example, the signal was moved to 'stop', the red glass would be shifted to appear in front of the lantern. One of the more tedious jobs was that of the lamp man, or more often boy, who had to refill the oil lamps every day, trudging for long distances down the track to climb up and down every signal.

▼ A lamp boy, whose job was to make sure that every signal had a fully filled oil lamp for use at night.

…e Yarmouth & Norwich line, which saw the …troduction of a system that separated trains …atially instead of by time. The line was divided … into blocks, each controlled by one signalman. …o train could enter a block until the previous train …d cleared it. The basis of the modern system was …w in place. A signalman in his box could receive …essages from others down the line, by means …f a coded system of bells sent by the telegraph. …hrough levers in the box attached by wires and …lleys to the signals themselves, he could control …l the signals in his block, and later this was …tended to controlling points. It was hard work … the early days: it required considerable effort to …ove a distant signal and shift points, though the …b was eased in later years with the introduction …f hydraulic systems. The signalman's job was …nely but carried great responsibility. It also had its …wards. There was a rapport between train crew …d signalmen. A friendly wave as a train went past …as not just a way of making human contact, it …assured the crew that the man in the box had not …en anything amiss as they went by.

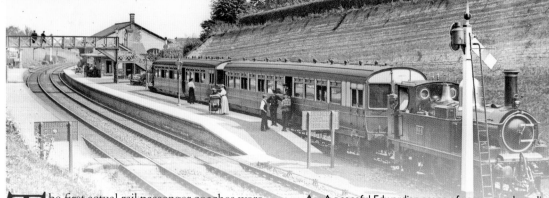

The first actual rail passenger coaches were reserved for those travelling first class, and were little more than stagecoaches set on flanged wheels. Open trucks continued to be used for third class, mostly without seats, until an accident on Christmas Eve 1842, when third-class passengers were in trucks attached to a goods train. The train ran into a landslip: eight passengers died and 17 were seriously injured. A law was promoted by the MP William Ewart Gladstone and passed in 1844 which stated that all companies had to provide at least one train a day in both directions, with covered compartments for third class at a rate of one penny (½p) per mile. The decision had a knock-on effect: if the second-class passengers were going to pay more then third class, then they expected more for their money. They wanted proper carriages with upholstered seats.

▲ A peaceful Edwardian scene of passengers boarding a local stopping train at Newnham in the Severn valley. Even though this is no main-line express, the little tank engine is immaculate with shining brass.

▼ London's Paddington station packed with bustling passengers in the rush hour in 1929.

A SOOTY SOLUTION

The improvements in third-class travel had an unfortunate side effect as far as the railway companies were concerned. As a Victorian writer expressed it, 'certain persons in superior positions' were base enough to travel in third-class carriages. The Manchester & Leeds Railway apparently had the answer. They reserved a third-class compartment for these 'better classes' – but before the train was made ready they paid a chimney sweep to empty his bag of soot in it!

ADDED COMFORTS

By the middle of the 19th century all passengers had at least a cover over their heads, but rail travel for many was still far from comfortable. In winter, passengers huddled under blankets or hired foot warmers at the station to keep warm. The Midland Railway led the way in making improvements.

▲ Children on a Swindon works outing to the seaside. Many large companies organized special excursion trains for the workers and their families.

EXCURSIONS

Railway travel was becoming something that could actually be enjoyed, rather than endured, for all types of passengers, and people began going on rail excursions. As early as 1841 Thomas Cook had arranged an excursion train from Leicester to Loughborough, taking 500 passengers to a temperance meeting for a return fare of one shilling (5p) for adults and sixpence (2½p) for children. It was the start of a successful rail excursion empire that was eventually to take passengers around the globe.

Rail travel changed many places forever. For example, when the railway reached Blackpool in 1846 it was little more than a village, but within half a century it had become the main holiday resort for industrial Lancashire, and each summer brought in the crowds. Seaside resorts had been places for wealthy tourists until the railways introduced the masses.

In 1875 they abolished second class altogether, making all existing second-class coaches into third class. They introduced a new class of six-wheel carriages, with four first-class compartments, usually five third class and a luggage compartment. The third-class compartments had seats stuffed with horsehair and covered with rough cloth, while first class enjoyed sprung seats with winged sides, like comfortable armchairs. The carriages were described at the time as 'lofty', which simply meant that, unlike earlier versions, it was possible to stand up straight in them. An improvement that the passengers did not see, but whose effects they certainly felt, was the introduction of wheels mounted on sprung bogies which were pivoted, unlike the old fixed axles. This produced a much smoother ride.

▲ An 1893 Midland Railway poster for Blackpool, a resort that developed thanks to the railway. The famous Blackpool tower had not yet been built.

The Midland Railway once again led the way in providing a new standard of luxury travel when the General Manager, Sir James Allport, introduced the first American Pullman coach to Britain in 1874. It was quite magnificent by the standards of the day, boasting an oil-fired stove and hot-water pipes to heat the carriages; efficient Argand lamps instead of smoky oil lamps; and running water for toilets and wash basins. Instead of rows of seats in closed compartments the carriage was open from end to end and passengers sat in plush swivel armchairs. The decor was equally grand, with embellished

▲ A line drawing of the interior of a Midland Railway Pullman coach. Designed by an American, George Mortimer Pullman, the coaches not only had luxurious furnishings but they also offered comfortable rides as they were mounted on well-sprung bogies with rubber shock absorbers.

◄ A 1920s poster for the Harrogate Pullman service. By this date Pullman coaches had been redesigned as cars where you could sit through the whole journey and be served with meals, without having to go to a separate dining car.

oilcloth and gilding. Soon after the first coach had proved a success the Midland ran a special train from St Pancras in London to Bradford in Yorkshire, consisting of five Pullman-type coaches and passengers enjoyed a whole new experience. They could stroll easily from one end of the train to the other. Pullman trains became synonymous with a better class of travel. Some had sleeping cars, but even the day coaches were special, with passengers having tables in front of their seats where they could be served meals.

CONTINENTAL LINKS

Pullman coaches had also been adopted by the most famous luxury train service in the world: the Orient Express. Britain was finally given a direct link in 1926, when a new service, the *Flèche d'Or*, was introduced between Dover and Paris, linked by overnight ferry to the English equivalent, the

considerable profit to be made by building their own hotels. By the early years of the 20th century they ran the biggest hotel chain in Britain, 79 of them in all, employing thousands of staff. Some, such as the Gleneagles in Edinburgh and the Adelphi in Liverpool, became famous: the latter was often spoken of as the grandest hotel in Britain outside London. But none was ever grander than the hotel at St Pancras station, designed for the Midland Railway by Sir George Gilbert Scott in an exuberant Gothic style. Opened to its first guests in 1873, it had 300 rooms, including suites with lavish displays of gold leaf on the walls and fires constantly burning in the grates. What they did not have was any sort of en suite bathrooms, so an army of servants was constantly scuttling around the corridors with chamber pots and tubs of hot water. The guests did not even have to climb the grand main staircase, but could take advantage of the new hydraulic 'ascending chambers' or, as we now call them, lifts. In its day it was the height of modernity as well as the epitome of luxury. In 2011 the hotel was restored to its former glory.

▲ Dining car services on luxury trains prided themselves on the quality of their meals: this imposing GWR chef would no doubt be equally at home in the kitchen of a five-star hotel.

Golden Arrow, between Dover and London. This meant that passengers could board coaches that were the epitome of elegance in London and stay in them for the Channel crossing and all the way through to Paris. They could also enjoy the very best service, including food prepared by chefs recruited from some of Europe's finest restaurants.

RAILWAY HOTELS

Those who travelled on these trains paid a premium, and they expected everything connected with their rail journeys to be of the same high standard. Important stations had special waiting rooms for first-class passengers, where the seats were comfortable and porters ensured there was always a blazing fire in the grate in winter. Passengers also often needed to stop overnight, preferably close to the station. The railway companies soon realized that there was a

▲ The Midland Railway Hotel at St Pancras station was arguably the most luxurious of all railway hotels. This is the grand staircase, restored to its full Victorian splendour as part of a 21st-century renovation programme.

Luxury trains and dashing expresses represent the romantic image of railway life, but railways were first built to serve industries. The earliest lines, serving mines and quarries, often ran on steep winding tracks from mine to river or port, running downhill fully loaded, sometimes with a horse riding in its own special truck, ready to haul the empties back uphill. One of these connected the Welsh slate mines and quarries of Blaenau Ffestiniog to the harbour at Port Madoc (Porthmadog). In 1862 the company's engineer, Charles Spooner, decided that the time had arrived to start using locomotives, but there was a problem to be faced: instead of being the standard gauge of 4ft 8½ins (1.42m) the rails were only 23½ ins (0.6m) apart.

NARROW-GAUGE RAILWAYS

The little engines devised for the track were the first to be used on a narrow-gauge railway, but the line soon became popular with passengers who appreciated the drama of a journey through the mountains of Snowdonia. More power was needed, but how did you get more power when the line was so narrow and twisty? The answer was the Double Fairlie, the 'push-me-pull-you' of the railway world, designed by Robert Francis Fairlie. With a cab in the middle, it looked like two engines that had been joined together, back to back. But the secret of its success was that the two boilers were

independently mounted, so that on a sharp bend one set of wheels might point one way and the other set in the opposite direction.

Narrow-gauge railways proved popular as the servants of many industries. For the crew they often represented a very different experience from working on any other sort of line. On the Ffestiniog line, for example, the ascent is steep so

▲ Collieries were the first industrial users of steam locomotives and continued to be important, many of them owning their own locomotives and rolling stock. This pithead scene at Featherstone in West Yorkshire shows loaded trucks with two typical tank engines in the background.

▼ The Ffestiniog Railway was the first narrow-gauge line to use steam locomotives. It introduced the unique Double Fairlie locomotives, seen here hauling a train between the slate mines and quarries of Blaenau Ffestiniog and the harbour at Port Madoc.

Bass Brewery at Burton-on-Trent had its own extensive rail network. This illustration shows trucks outside the large ale and hop store in the early 1890s.

that the little engines have to work hard and the fireman scarcely has time to rest. Going down, life becomes altogether easier on the footplate as the engine acts as a brake rather than as motive power. There may not be much variety when going up and down the same length of track all day every day, but there is compensation in the magnificent scenery. The Ffestiniog line has always been a great favourite with steam devotees. Perhaps the most famous of all express drivers from the age of steam was Bill Hoole. On his death in 1979, he chose to be buried in a cemetery close to the Ffestiniog tracks. His gravestone reads: 'BILL HOOLE – ENGINEMAN EXTRAORDINARY'.

COMING DOWN THE MOUNTAIN

Many years ago it was possible to pay for a ride in one of the trucks of the slate railway at Talyllyn in rural Wales, opened in 1866, to enjoy a picnic at the top of the mountain. You could keep the truck with you and, when it was time to go home, jump in, release the brake and roll back down the hill. Modern health and safety rules clearly did not apply in those days. Today visitors to the Talyllyn Railway can enjoy a ride on the historic line that runs for 7¼ miles (11.6km) through the Fathew valley.

When their working days ended, many of these small lines found a new life carrying tourists and steam enthusiasts.

BUILT FOR BREWERIES

By no means were all industrial lines narrow gauge. Many large companies had their own internal rail system, with their own locomotives and rolling stock. The brewing industry of Burton-on-Trent, Staffordshire, became hugely dependent on the rail network: at the peak of production in the 1880s it was sending out 3 million barrels of beer a year. The biggest of these Burton breweries was Bass, whose trade was so important to the Midland Railway that when they came to build their London terminus at St Pancras the undercroft was built with the supports set apart so that three barrels would exactly sit between them. The brewery also had its own private rail system, with 16 miles (25km) of track, the longest of its kind in the country. They had ten locomotives, hustling backwards and forwards, taking out full barrels and returning empties and transporting raw material.

The agricultural industry came to rely heavily on the railways, particularly in distributing milk. Scenes such as this, with milk churns being loaded, were common in the early years of the 20th century.

GOING UNDERGROUND

◄ The opening of the Metropolitan Railway in London in 1863, the world's first underground railway. The engineer, John Fowler, in the foreground and wearing the white top hat, has a smile on his face, obviously happy with his work.

▼ Parts of the Metropolitan line ran in the open. This illustration show two trains crossing, and the depth of the line can be gauged from the traffic passing on the road bridge up above.

Underground railways are a familiar part of many city transport systems, but the pioneering lines were very different from those we have today. The first, the Metropolitan Railway, was built in London and was designed to link the main-line stations of Paddington, Euston and King's Cross. The line was not, strictly speaking, in a tunnel but was constructed by digging a deep cutting, then building a cover over the top of it. It opened in 1863 – long before the development of electric trains – and all the carriages were hauled by steam locomotives. It was a huge success, with over 30,000 passengers crowding to take this novel form of transport on the first day. By the end of the first year some 10 million passengers had used the line. Although the engineer, John Fowler, had designed engines that created as little smoke and steam as possible, there was no disguising the fact that the trains were dirty. Victorian gentlemen on the way to their city offices were not pleased to find their immaculate shirts spotted with smuts, nor were ladies happy to be seen wearing grubby lace.

THE CABLE SYSTEM

Another engineer, Peter Barlow, came up with an alternative system. His railway, opened in 1870, ran in a circular tunnel, just 6ft 8in (2.02m) in diameter, under the Thames between Tower Hill and Southwark. Passengers were taken up and down in a steam-powered lift, after which they

▲ A drawing of Stockwell station on the City & Suburban Railway in 1890. The carriages seen on the right with their high, narrow windows were so claustrophobic they became known as 'padded cells'.

climbed high up the walls, leaving narrow slits for windows. The company had decided that as there was nothing to see underground nothing else was needed, but the carriages were stuffy and were soon nicknamed the 'padded cells'.

The new system required a complete rethink of existing railway practice. A new safety device was introduced for drivers, known as the dead man's handle. The driver had to keep pressure on the handle at all times – if he took his hand away the power automatically cut off.

ot into a small car for the trip under the river and ere hauled along by cable worked by two small eam engines. It was very inexpensive: passengers uld make the one-way trip for just a penny (½p), t the cables kept jamming. It was all dismantled: airs were built to replace the lifts and people had walk rather than ride through to the other side. owever, that was not the end of the use of cables r underground railways. They were used on the cottish District Subway in Glasgow that opened 1896 and ran as a 6½-mile (10.5-km) loop that ossed the River Clyde twice. The cable system mained in use until the 1930s.

MOVE TO ELECTRICITY

eam was never really going to be the answer for nderground railways, and there was a successful ecedent to follow. In 1883 an enterprising ntrepreneur called Magnus Volk began operating n electric railway at Brighton, East Sussex. It still ns today, giving holidaymakers a ride along the afront at a stately 10mph (16kph). When London ot its second underground railway – the City & outh London – it was a genuine tube line, and the ecision was taken to power it by electricity. It was pened in 1890 by the Prince of Wales (later ing Edward VII) and at once proved its periority to steam. But the system was far from erfect. The carriages, like modern tube trains, ad benches along both sides, but the upholstery

▲ The City & Suburban Railway in the 1920s, with a typical electric locomotive of the time. The 'padded cells' have been replaced by more conventional carriages.

CELEBRATING 150 YEARS

The year 2013 marks the 150th anniversary of the opening of the first part of the London Underground, from Paddington to Farringdon. Test runs in 2012 in preparation for the event saw steam trains pulling into London Underground stations after close of normal service, to the amazement of late-night onlookers.

THE RAILWAY WORKS

▲ The GWR established their works in 1843 on what was then a green field site near the little town of Swindon. This photograph shows the engine repair shop in 1908.

➤ Swindon works in 1927, showing the first of the King class express locomotives under construction.

As soon as the railway system began to develop it was realized that companies would need somewhere to build and service locomotives and rolling stock. The first engineering works were built at Shildon, County Durham, on the Stockton & Darlington line, where in 1826 the engineer Timothy Hackworth began work with just 20 men. It was all very primitive at first. The only artificial light was provided by candles and there were no machine tools, just hand lathes and screw jacks for lifting. In time, a new railway village developed where once there had only been four houses and 'a wet, swampy field', according to the original surveyor.

SETTING THE PATTERN

Far grander projects were begun by other companies that set the pattern for railway works and towns. The Great Western Railway chose a site next to the tiny market town of Swindon in Wiltshire for their works. By 1844 there were facilities for repairing and building locomotives as well as a foundry for casting the different parts. By 1860 there was a rolling mill for making iron rails, and large numbers of Welsh workers, who had experience in this kind of work, were recruited. The carriage works were added eight years later. By this time Swindon was one of the country's largest engineering works, equipped with all the latest machine tools and demanding the highest levels of precision workmanship.

Very early on in the development it was obvious that the old town could never hold the expanding workforce, and New Swindon was developed as a model village, consisting of neat terraces of stone cottages, well spaced out. The company set new standards of welfare. In 1855 they built the Mechanics' Institute, with a large hall for meetings and concerts, classrooms and a library. It is a measure of just how forward-thinking the company was that Swindon did not get a public library until 1943. Many of the big railway companies were equally enlightened, providing all kinds of public buildings. At Crewe in Cheshire, for example, where the Grand Junction Railway established works in 1843, one of their first tasks was to build a new church, which incorporated cast-iron pillars made at the works.

AN ARMY OF RAILWAY WORKERS

Alfred Williams described the start of the working day at Swindon in his book *Life in a Railway Factory*, published in 1915: 'As soon as the ten minutes hooter sounds the men come teeming out of the various parts of the town in great numbers, and by five minutes to six the streets leading to the entrances are packed with a dense crowd of men and boys … It is a mystery where they all come from. Ten thousand workmen! They are like an army pressing forward to battle. Tramp! Tramp! Tramp! Still they pour down the streets with the regularity of trained soldiers.'

▲ The GWR had to build a whole town, Swindon New Town, to house its workforce. This photograph shows houses after they had been refurbished in the 1970s, but they are still basically as they were when first built in the 1840s and 50s.

A WEALTH OF EXPERTISE

The great railway companies relied on their chief engineers, from Robert Stephenson (1803–59) who built the famous *Rocket* to Sir Nigel Gresley (1876–1941) who designed the record-breaking *Mallard,* to provide them with the finest steam locomotives. But they were equally reliant on the expertise and craftsmanship of the workforce, who did everything from forging massive connecting rods to sewing the upholstery for the carriages. The working areas where they carried out their wide variety of tasks ranged from those where boilers were riveted, producing a literally deafening cacophony, to the carriage works that were havens of peace by comparison. The machinery was expensive – and anyone found neglecting or damaging a machine would be instantly dismissed, and even minor offences could lead to the loss of a day's pay. The penalties were harsh, but they ensured that standards were among the highest of any industry in the land.

▲ The forge at Swindon: connecting rods are being shaped from steel ingots using a powerful steam hammer.

➤ Swindon made virtually everything that the railway needed. These women are weaving netting that will be used for making luggage racks for carriages.

RAILWAY DISASTERS

The very first fatal railway accident occurred during the opening ceremony of the Liverpool & Manchester Railway in 1830. A train had stopped and the local MP, William Huskisson, stepped out onto the track to greet the Duke of Wellington. No one was yet used to the speed of locomotives: people cried out that *Rocket* was approaching but Huskisson was too slow to move; the engine hit him and he died of his injuries.

THE CLAYTON TUNNEL TRAGEDY

Some drivers on the early locomotives were keen to put them though their paces and were frustrated by the safety valves that stopped them applying extra steam pressure. They unwisely tied the valves down, and the inevitable result was an exploding boiler. But there were many things that could go wrong in a system as complex as the railways. Obstacles on the track or poor track maintenance could cause

▼ The accident at Staplehurst in 1865, caused by a collapsing bridge. Charles Dickens was in one of the carriages that can be seen still on the embankment.

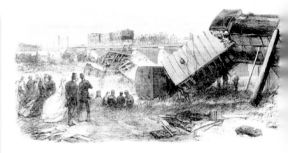

HEROIC DICKENS

A modest bridge at Staplehurst in Kent was under repair when it gave way under an express train on 9 June 1865. One of the passengers, sharing a compartment with two ladies, was Charles Dickens. Their carriage was tilted over but remained on the track. He told his companions, 'We can't help ourselves, but we can be quiet and composed', to which the elder one replied with true British phlegm: 'Thank you. Rely upon me. Upon my soul I will be quiet.' They emerged unscathed – others were less fortunate: ten people were killed and 49 injured, some of whom were helped by Dickens. The accident affected him badly: writing to a friend about the incident four days later, he ended the letter, 'I feel the shake and am obliged to stop.'

derailments, often with dramatic results. However, most of the really bad disasters came when trains ran into each other. One of the worst occurred in 1861, when three trains were following each other down the line from London to Brighton, with only seven minutes separating all three. Due to a mix up over signals, the second train was stopped in Clayton tunnel (in West Sussex) and the third train ploughed straight into the back of it: 23 passengers died and 176 were seriously injured. At least some good came out of the tragedy, as it led directly to an improvement in safety systems.

◄ A spectacular derailment: the GWR broad-gauge locomotive *Rob Roy* came off the tracks near Gloucester in 1868 and attracted a lot of interested spectators.

► The scene of carnage at Thorpe in 1874, when two trains were involved in a head-on collision.

THE THORPE DISASTER

Driving into the back of other trains was bad enough, but the events at Thorpe, Norfolk, on the Great Eastern Railway in 1874 were, if anything, worse. Part of the line was single track, and in theory there should have been a foolproof system to ensure that only one train at a time was on that section. But on the night of 10 September there was a terrible mix-up: with confused instructions and poor visibility in driving rain, two trains were sent hurtling towards each other. No one could tell the enquiry exactly what happened in the last moments as both train crews died in the collision, but one driver must at least have seen what was about to happen and tried his best to prevent it: his regulator was shut and the brake screwed hard down. That night, 25 lives were lost and 73 people were injured.

THE BRIDGE OVER THE RIVER TAY

Another accident was immortalized in the words of William McGonagall, notorious for his excruciatingly bad verse:

> *Beautiful Railway Bridge of the Silv'ry Tay!*
> *Alas, I am very sorry to say*
> *That ninety lives have been taken away*
> *On the last Sabbath day of 1879,*
> *Which will be remembered for a very long time.*

The bridge over the River Tay was the longest in Britain when it collapsed on that stormy night, and the subsequent inquiry found that it was all due to fundamental design flaws. It was the last to be built of iron: future bridges would use steel instead. Although rail travel is one of the safest means of transport ever developed, inevitably accidents still occur.

▲ The aftermath of the collapse of the Tay bridge in 1879: a steam launch and divers' barge are seen here engaged in the search, but there were no survivors.

A sign of things to come: the GWR diesel railcar No.1 seen at Reading station in the 1930s, next to one of the giants of the steam age, the locomotive *King Edward VII*.

The last steam locomotive to be built for British Rail: *Evening Star* being named by Dr Beeching in 1960.

Throughout the 19th century, the steam locomotive ruled the railways of Britain. As the 20th century dawned, it seemed that steam's triumph was assured when on 9 May 1904 the Ocean Mail train, headed by GWR's *City of Truro*, passed the magic figure of 100mph (160kph). It was steam that gave the railways its sense of glamour, and the men who controlled them were regarded as heroes. However, the truth was that for all its splendour the steam locomotive was not very efficient and the black smoke pouring from countless chimneys on the engines was a serious cause of pollution. Alternatives had already appeared before the Victorian age came to an end. The first electric locomotive, designed by the German engineer Werner von Siemens, was demonstrated at the Berlin Trade Exhibition as early as 1879. At first its use was mainly limited to the underground system and, in the years before there was a national grid, rail companies were not too keen to go to the expense of building their own power stations. But another German inventor had an alternative to offer.

DAYS OF DIESEL

In 1892 Rudolf Diesel took out an English patent for his new internal combustion engine. It was not immediately obvious how it could be adapted for use on rails, but in the 1930s the first diesel railcars came into service. Once again Germany led the way in spectacular fashion with the 'Flying Hamburger' – a speedy railcar that immediately began recording faster times than the famous British express the 'Cheltenham Flyer'. The 1930s were to see the first steps in Britain of moving away from the steam age, with the start of electrification and the introduction of handsome new diesel railcars. The advantages were obvious. The crew of steam locomotives had to arrive early to prepare the train; the driver of a railcar had simply to get into the cab and turn a key. The problem of smoke pollution was greatly

▶ The scrap yard at Barry Island which became a graveyard for old steam locomotives. It was from here that the railway preservation societies got many of the locomotives that they restored and which are still running today.

▼ The romance of the steam railways lives on. This little engine is on the Talyllyn Railway, the first to be taken over and run by volunteers.

reduced as well. Modernization was on the programme, but everything was held up by the outbreak of war in 1939.

POST-WAR RAILWAYS

After the Second World War, there were two main problems to be solved: how to modernize an ageing stock of locomotives, and how to make a system designed for the Victorian era pay in the age of motor cars and trucks. In 1960 the last locomotive to be built for the newly nationalized railways was rolled out of the Swindon works and named *Evening Star*. In 1963 the chairman of British Railways, Dr Richard Beeching, issued his famous – or to many enthusiasts, infamous – report. It called for the wholesale closure of uneconomic branch lines. In the 1960s some 5,000 miles (8,000km) of track were shut and over 3,000 stations closed. It seemed as if the days of steam trains chuffing along romantic little branch lines had gone forever. However, enthusiasts were soon heading to Wales and the locomotive graveyard at the Barry scrap yard, buying up the old engines to run again on restored lines. Thanks to their efforts we can still enjoy the golden age of the steam railways.

The following museums specialize in railways or have important railway collections. Contact the sites or visit their websites for further information, including opening dates and times. Details of Britain's preserved railways can be found at www.heritagerailways.com.

Beamish: the Living Museum of the North, Beamish, County Durham DH9 0RG

Bressingham Steam and Gardens, Low Road, Bressingham, Diss, Norfolk IP22 2AA

Colonel Stephens Railway Museum, The John Miller Building, Tenterden Town Station, Station Road, Tenterden, Kent TN30 6HE

Crewe Heritage Centre, Vernon Way, Crewe, Cheshire CW1 2DB

Didcot Railway Centre, Didcot, Oxfordshire OX11 7NJ

Head of Steam – Darlington Railway Museum, Station Road, Darlington, County Durham DL3 6ST

London Transport Museum, Covent Garden Piazza, London WC2E 7BB

Midland Railway – Butterley, Butterley Station, Ripley, Derbyshire DE5 3QZ

Museum of Science and Industry, Liverpool Road, Castlefield, Manchester M3 4FP

National Railway Museum at Shildon, Shildon, County Durham DL4 1PQ

▲ A semaphore signal set at stop at Rannoch Moor in Scotland, one of Britain's loneliest railway stations.

National Railway Museum, Leeman Road, York YO26 4XJ

National Waterfront Museum, Oystermouth Road, Marine Quarter, Swansea SA1 3RD

Riverside Museum: Scotland's Museum of Transport and Travel, 100 Pointhouse Place, Glasgow G3 8AS

Steam (Museum of the Great Western Railway), Kemble Drive, Swindon, Wiltshire SN2 2TA

Stephenson Railway Museum, Middle Engine Lane, North Shields, Tyne & Wear NE29 8DX

Information correct at time of going to press.

▲ A family on the footplate of *Caerphilly Castle* at Steam, Swindon.

▲ The *Duchess of Hamilton* at the National Railway Museum in York.